1

MW01503600

OF THE SOUL

by

G. Shanier

to Always Remember to follow Your Spirit and flow with the natural energies

*G. Shanier
(Gloria S. Clarke)
Nov 1998*

ISBN: 0-7392-0002-X

Printed in the USA by

MORRIS PUBLISHING
3212 East Highway 30 · Kearney, NE 68847 · 1-800-650-7888

DEDICATION

This book is dedicated to all of the
beautiful
Spirits who helped make this book
possible.

May they always live within my heart.

LOVE TALES

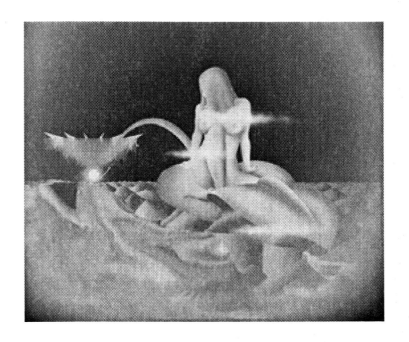

OF THE SOUL

PREFACE
Our Journey in Life

Throughout your journey in life, always remember that love, in the truest sense of the word, knows no bounds. It is totally free and giving without *expecting* anything in return. It is joyous onto itself and cares without caring about outcomes. It gives of itself unconditionally and without manipulation.

Honest love will lend a guiding hand to help someone grow within him/herself, and will understand and be filled with joy if that person's path and journey in life leads towards an avenue away from one of union for the two of you. Love has no concept of the word jealousy and knows no possessiveness. Love loves from Love itself and doesn't try to control. It is incapable of holding another person responsible for it's own happiness, for it's happiness is generated from within.

Love does not form an ideal, fantasy image and then try to mold another being into that image for it's own self-satisfaction. Nor does love project a false image as a form of gaining another's attention. Love knows and understands that even though honesty *can* hurt the Ego, deception damages the Spirit.

I was once asked to describe the differences, if any, between being in love with nature and life, and being in love with another person. For myself, the differences are nominal; When I'm outside with Nature, I can truly be in-the-moment, without having to contend with surface facades. I'm totally open and free to receive all of the energies offered, and free to give energy back to Nature with no strings attached;

no conditions. It doesn't matter if it turns cold, the wind kicks up, or pours rain. I accept it all and feel exhilarated. But, if I get to the point where I have had enough of the elements, I still accept it, but am free to find shelter anytime I want. I feel total freedom and pure joy, combined with a surrealistic sense of serenity. The free-flowing exchange of energies make me feel so powerful, I could accomplish anything.

When I'm around the person with whom I am in love, I feel exactly the same way. The only differences are the physical sharing of life's experiences, the verbal communications, and the magical physical union between two people, which intensifies all other feelings. And, like my love for life and nature, my love for another being is akin to energy; it can never be destroyed; it simply changes form.

It is my hope that the reader will be able to see him/herself in my writings, or possibly learn to let go of the surface facades for awhile, and experience the magnificent beauty of life itself that surrounds all of us on a daily basis.

This book is a celebration of Life and Love to . . . *seek within and flow without.*

G. Shanier, Columbia Falls, M.T.

CONTENTS

SECTION I

SPIRITUAL UNION

AND RECOGNITION

OF

LOVE FLOWING WITHIN

Throughout my life I could feel you there,
    waiting to connect;
Worlds apart across the earth,
    looking for the right track.

The one to bring me to the right place
    so that we may meet,
To join in bodies and in minds,
    so the venture would be complete.

We have our obstacles to overcome
    as we go along our way,
But every one strengthens the bond between us
    and generates power with each passing day.

I know the Lord has a plan,
    by giving us this burden to bear,
But once we pass this ultimate test
    the rest of the way will be clear.

Souvenirs of our moments together
　　keep dancing in my mind;
Creating a kaleidoscope of feelings
　　that extend to the end of time.

The dancing rainbow of energy
　　gives them a life of their own,
To play hide-n-seek from conscious thought
　　or make their presence well known.

Even while gliding
　　through the essence of my thoughts,
They delve deep into my total being,
　　ever aware and never lost.

They mingle with the present
　　to always remain in the moment
And then become the present;
　　by riding the waves of energy from which
the love grows.

Many times the woods are kind
and fill me with moments of joy.
Other times they're not so kind,
and fill me with myself instead.

The sun was bright and radiating warmth
as I entered the woods' secret passage;
Suggesting the promise of exhilarating energy,
with no hint of the sorrow ahead.

The final stage of my cleansing
was waiting along the path;
The one to make me face the greatest pain
that would seem to tear my heart in half.

My friends, the woods, knew I had no choice
        and buried the consequences within me;
They knew I had to face the pain
        before I could ever set it free.

To create and nurture a brand new life
        with the man I truly love,
Is the one miracle I want the most
        and know I can never have.

Maybe the woods thought they were being kind
        when I became pregnant within their midst,
And felt the life growing inside me
        and the touch of your fingertips.

You were standing there before me
        with tears of love forming in your eyes,
And as you reach out to feel the baby move,
        it turned like the ocean tide.

The experience was so incredibly real
        that it took my breath away,
And left me crying with broken heart,
        when it ended as fast as it came.

What wonder I felt when I looked in your eyes
 on that magical night we met.
I felt my spirit leap to join yours
 to form a life-long bond.

Your dazzling smile radiated warmth,
 as you extended your welcome.
And somehow, I forgot everything else
 as I reveled in the feeling of being where I
belong.

Feelings of confusion and mystification consumed me,
 as I felt compelled to linger.
Not wanting to leave your protective bubble,
 I felt my steps falter to make the moment last
longer.

For the presence I saw in you overwhelmed my
existence,
 as you became a flow of blue and gold light;
Sending forth so much energy
 I thought I might be blinded by the sight.

The meeting was brief, but so ever powerful
 that I remember every detail to this day,
Still feeling confused and mystified,
 by the friendship that eventually would come
my way.

The words you read upon the page
　　　express the love my lips cannot convey.
They tell the story of my life since we met,
　　　in a creative way I hope you can accept.

Without you, the page would be blank;
　　　the words scrambled in my mind,
Hanging in limbo just as they had
　　　in so many years gone by.

Your presence inspired my Soul
　　　and set the words free,
To flow together in beautiful prose,
　　　as a special gift from me.

I'm sitting here, staring at the blank page with so
many thoughts running through my head.
Expressions of thankfulness for the love you've given
seem to escape me.
The sheer power I feel when your eyes probe mine-
The sense I get that the smallest gesture contains the
totality of your being;
that you are giving of yourself completely and
honestly.
Words cannot describe the way I treasure and
cherish every moment we spend together, or the way
I appreciate you.
Never before have I experienced a love like yours -
Powerful and free, and full of tenderness.
You gave to me what no one else has ---
Honesty and truthfulness.
Acceptance and pride shines through your eyes when
you see me walk in the room.
The power of the universe could not possibly explain
the depth of feeling I get from you and have for you.
Your presence is forever with me in everything I do,
making me feel warm and protected, even though
you're not here.
You roam freely in my dreams, full of passion and
shimmering energy,
letting me know you are always near,
for time and distance have no meaning when two
hearts meet.

The softness of your spirit
    speaks of an inner strength,
That radiates into the outer world
    and adds stability in it's wake.

Your quiet depth of feeling
    whispers loudly through your eyes,
Conveying more communication
    than words could ever explain.

Your energy dances and glimmers
    with the sparkle in your eyes,
And penetrates the moment
    with excitement and surprise.

The beauty and freedom
    contained within your love,
Sets my soul singing
    and the passion reeling
As I gaze upon you once again.

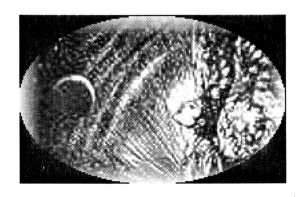

"What's this?" I heard a voice say
    when our eyes met the very first time.
"I see a web of power and energy
    reaching out to connect with mine.
There's a door opening in the web
    inviting me to come in,
Offering warmth and many experiences
    with a hint of a mischievous grin.

Can this beauty really be real,
    or is it just a hallucination?
To see so much depth in just a glance
    makes me tingle with anticipation."
A single strand of energy
    then shot out and lodged in my being
Planting the seed of what was to be,
    with many moments yet unseen.

The cool winter breeze on my face
reminds me of the gentleness of your touch.
It's coolness brushes my cheek ever so lightly
and sends chills down my spine with a hush.

My body feels exhilarated and full of energy
when I feel the lightness of winter's kiss,
Which sends me reeling back to the way
you caress my spirit with your fingertips.

The cold winter air catches my breath
and causes tears to form in my eyes,
Just like the slightest glimpse of your radiance
catches my breath and fills me with tears of
happiness.

The brisk mountain air brings a bright
rosy glow to my face,
While the memory of your love and tenderness
creates a glowing flush in it's place.

The sparkling stars on a clear, cold night
mirror the stars I see in your smile -
And just like I treasure the beauty of winter,
so I also treasure the beauty of you!

So many months ago
        when I said I loved you as a friend,
The power of the words
        opened up a river that will never end.

I didn't realize then
        just how deep the river flowed,
Until I discovered I had given my heart
        and felt my spirit glow.

I give my love unconditionally
        and with no expectations.
For I swore I'd never hurt you
        and there'd be no solicitations.

I will never ask questions or make demands,
        for love in the truest sense is free.
I'm happy living my life
        in a way that's right for me;

By loving you silently
        and allowing the Spirit to direct
Whatever is meant to be.

The fibers of our being
        have permeated the air.
Sending energy in all directions,
        knowing the touch will always be there.

Time and distance have no meaning
        in this kaleidoscope of sound;
The rainbows sing and stars keep healing,
        as the universe spins 'round and 'round.

The majestic radiance of the connection
        has opened doors unknown
Extending an invitation to be enveloped
        within the warmth of the vibrational tones.

The wonderment of beauty
        transcends us into a dance of awe;
Mingling with the glitter of stardust
        as we respond to the mystical call.

The long awaited joyous reunion
        is just within our reach,
When the golden shimmer of harmonies
        lead us to our island of retreat.

The love we share contains the power of the eagle
    and the beauty of the rose.
It landed upon a branch of energy
    that was accompanied by a single cone.

The depth of feeling intertwined and mingled
    to form an instant bond,
Gaining incredible height and speed
    while remaining firmly rooted in the ground.

We are kept apart in this physical realm
    because of separate lives and paths,
But like the eagle attracted to the beauty of the rose,
    it returns to gaze upon it's softness
Ever knowing it may never land.

When I say, "I believe in you,"
        do you know what it is I believe?
It's not a dream image I created
        in hopes it would never leave,
                AND
It's not believing in the thought
        of what you can do for me,
As a way of escaping reality.

I believe in you being true to yourself
        and listening to the song of your heart.

To believe in someone is to see inside their being
        and catch the depth of their honesty,
Believing they are following their chosen path,
        being led by the light of their dreams and
destiny.

Believing in you means I accept the love you have to
offer
        without making it more or less than it really is,
By freely giving love energy in return
        and allowing it to fill me with joyfulness.

Something has happened to my soul,
    that I simply can't explain.
It seems to have joined with my body and mind;
    they are now one and the same.

The dazzling sight of your spirit
    sets my body on fire.
Creating a tingling within my mind,
    intensifying my soul's desire.

You pull me into your being
    through a vortex of sound;
Displaying a kaleidoscope of energy
    and colors knowing no bounds.

The rhythm of your song is centered
    and resonates with a welcoming beat,
While my own melody sings in answer to it,
    offering a tranquil retreat.

The shadows of uncertainty consumed me
in ways better left unsaid.
Clouds covered the sun I was longing to see
and allowed the gremlins to run wild in my
head.

Surface conditions took over my being,
and I lost sight of true reality;
The one of our spirits merging and joining
within the realm of our chosen destiny.

I saw the longing on my mother's face,
as she raised me for 16 years,
Looking forward to the time she'd be able to embrace
her mate waiting patiently in a different sphere.

She scolded me as though I were a little girl
having a fit because I didn't get my way,
Reminding me, you and I are of the same world
and I would be wise to step back and cherish
the day.

She showed me how empty I felt inside
until that day our spirits met,
Asking if superfluous surface pride
was worth the price of being forced to forget.

**Which brings me to the present
and a very special request:**

*to please keep the doors open between us
and believe in me once again.*

When I first saw you so many months ago,
	your radiance filled the entire room.
I was transfixed by the sight before me
	and felt my own essence brighten it's glow.

But you were dancing with another
	and I installed the proverbial blocks,
So the energy flowing through me
	wouldn't reach out and give access to my
thoughts.

From the hundreds who were in the room,
	only you caught my eye that night;
And I was thinking how magnificent it would be,
	if a special friendship was within my sight.

I played it safe and stayed away,
	ignoring the presence that I saw,
Until that magic night we met,
	when I felt the blocks begin to fall.

The power and strength of the connection we felt
	is real, this I know,
But realize it'll never be restrictive or demanding,
	for it needs room in order to grow.

The kaleidoscope of energies are free to dance at
will;
        they can delve deep within each others' being,
Or simply watch
        from the windowsill.

With that, I invite you to come dance within my
timelessness,
        as you would dance on a ballroom floor,
Waltzing and twirling and dipping,
        until you think you can dance no more.

Explore my inner being
        as you would explore the surface under your
feet,
Tentative with the first few steps,
        to see if it's sticky or sleek.

Listen to the rhythm of my music,
        as you listen to the beat of a song,
Flowing free and effortlessly,
        knowing you can always return home.

My love for you has evolved,
     into something for which words don't exist.
It flows deeper than the imagination
     and reached the point it doesn't matter; it just
is.

It can never be a threat in any way,
     for it generates power within itself,
By giving energy and strength freely,
     with no thoughts of tomorrow or doubts.

It dances upon the fibers
     of many souvenirs shared,
And uses the rainbow of colors
     to weave songs of gossamer.

It cares without caring;
     that is the secret of it's strength.
It has learned to let go of the fear
     and focuses on total faith.

Like energy, my love can never be destroyed,
     for it has survived lifetimes past.
And even if we never kiss again,
     it's strength and power will continue to last.

Energizing solitude stimulates by mind,
into reveilles of the past and
melodies of a different kind.

The songs' distant experiences permeates my being,
creating endless roller-coaster rides
and understandings yet unseen.

I see an encouraging pink mist of love
forming a bubble around me,
catching a rhythm of wind from above
floating into treasures and harmonies.

The dancing kaleidoscope of memories
transforming into soothing radiance,
guide me through tranquil reflections
and a wonderment of joyfulness.

I bless and cherish each and every mark
knowing they helped form who I am today
and provided shelter against the dark,
as I traveled along my way.

Now, I cast my eyes on the present
and the serenity of the land
and tremble in anticipation,
of the dreams I'm still holding in my hands.

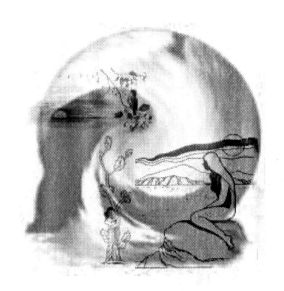

Flowing within time
  and becoming one with the spirit
Showed me the beauty of your soul.

The radiance of rainbow colors
  called to me like a beacon in the night,
Guiding me to your light.

I was enveloped in a cocoon of warmth
  as you opened your door
And invited me inside.

Your spirit embraced me with a passion
  I cannot describe.
And, as I felt my essence unite with yours,
  the pure sense of joy told me
I had nothing to hide.

And now, though our spirits
  are never apart,
They yearn to once again
  complete the union
Of mind, body and heart.

The pain of separation
  grows deeper everyday,
But from the pain comes a strength of love
  that will never be denied.

Magic was in the air
        the might our spirits meshed,
And space was charged with electricity
        when our eyes finally met.

Our Selves vibrated with joy
        at the physical connection,
For we had traveled down many paths
        in preparation for this moment.

We heard the rhythm of one another's song
        gently guiding our direction.
Separate and opposite, yet together,
        drawing us closer to where we belong.

When I looked into your eyes that first time,
        I was filled with wonder
At the incredible power and purity of your being.

And when you embraced me with
        an indescribable warmth and said,
"Friends for life," I felt our energies unite.

We are still continuing our separate journeys,
        but time and space have no meaning
For we are always together
        reveling in each other's growth.

I gave you my heart
     without ever being aware
Of the total joy I'd feel,
     even when we're apart.

It is yours to keep,
     if that is what you want,
Or you can give it back
     before it gets too deep.

Either way is okay
     for it makes no difference,
Because nothing will change
     what I'm feeling today.

We met when we did
     for reasons yet unknown,
But know my heart is true
     as it finds it's way back home

32

I met you in a dream
    as a radiant beam of light,
filled with peace, joy and kindness.
No words were spoken, but I knew you
    wanted me to join you.

You showed me the power and beauty
    of the mountains, valleys, river; nature-
You took me on a journey into life itself;
    one of timelessness;
One with no boundaries or surface facades
    to block the magic of the day.

We entered into the world of rituals
    and mythology.
You showed me the power and truth
    of each and every one.
By blending your energies with mine,
    you taught me how to feel the connection.
Through you, I felt the reality
    of even the smallest ritual.
I felt the connectedness and balance
    of the spiritual and physical worlds.

And, when I awoke, I looked around
    and discovered it wasn't a dream-
You were still there beside me,
    the scent of nature was still in the air,
And time had stood still.

You have my strength to lean on
      when your world gets rough.
I'll send you all the love I can
      and pray that it's enough.

My spirit sends energy to your soul
      when your own well seems almost dry -
I'll replenish what was lost
      and help bring the sparkle back to your eye.

The pain you feel is only momentary,
      even though it cuts so deep,
But know my love will help you heal
      without expectations or grief.

Just whisper my name
      and I'll be there beside you,
Caressing and loving with a shimmering touch,
      as light as the mornings' dew.

I knew the risk; I took the chance
and allowed myself to be enveloped in your being.
The beauty and radiance I experienced there
were unlike anything I had ever seen.

The total sense of freedom
flowed like a dam breaking from my soul,
And the feelings of love danced with utter delight
at being released from their inner hold.

Our spirits mingled and joined together
showering us with fibers;
Strengthening the bond of lives now past
as we walk into the future inspired.

What initially appeared to be brief in nature
has actually just begun;
For the doors have been opened between us
and our memories have merged as one.

Circumstances may keep us apart
and at times we may feel the pain,
But the overwhelming joy of what we already share
brings rainbows and sunshine in place of the rain.

Listen with your heart
And follow the beat of my song.
It'll take you into paradise
Within a world that's gone wrong.

Explore the depths of it's meaning
And the essence of it's timelessness -
Conveying the sense of power and freedom,
It's melody speaks to the center of your being.

Immerse yourself in the totality of it's power
And experience the kaleidoscope of sounds,
Taking you deeper and deeper into it's beauty,
Reassured you'll never drown.

Allow the radiant waves of light the rhythm creates
To dance upon your spirit,
Keeping you warm and safe from harm,
As your own song sings in answer to it.

How can I possibly convey
The depth of feeling I hold inside.
My soul has become totally exposed;
There's no need for it to hide.

I've given you the gift of my heart
Honestly and freely: it is yours.
You may keep it as long as you like,
Or simply return it and close the doors.

There will be no expectations
Or unspoken demands.
Only honesty on your part
Is all I'll ever ask.

But yet, you've already given me
More than I've ever known -
That's the respect of wanting to start clean,
So our love will have a chance to grow.

The journey of healing
Is rough, I know.
But it helps to visualize the pain as a bubble,
Bless it, and then let it go.

I'll be there in spirit
Whenever you call my name.
I'll help keep you focused
As you wade through those mental games.

Only the divine knows what lies ahead
As we live from day-to-day,
So I'll continue to cherish our moments together
Knowing you'll join me, in your own special way.

I want to express the respect and pride
I have for you inside.
Your journey took you down the roughest trail,
But your strength and courage prevailed.

I appreciate the struggle
You elected to forego;
One filled with turmoil and pain,
Demanding that you grow.

I see your power increasing
At a most impressive rate,
Directing it's brilliance and radiance
To break through the mighty gates.

Your energy is now flowing
Like a river running free;
It's rushing forward and gaining strength,
As the Divine intended it to be.

When the river merges with the ocean,
It's journey will finally be complete
And it's waters will flow in the freedom
Of the glorious and expansive retreat.

The fantasies you create when you're away
        are so vivid I wonder if they're real.
The feel of you is so strong inside me,
        I can feel your breath at the back of my neck.

While the touch of your fingertips send shivers
        down my spine
And the lingering taste of your sensitive lips
        remind me of a fine, sweet wine.

Your responsiveness causes the passion to swell
        to heights of incredible desire,
Filling my every need on every level,
        adding fuel to the blazing fire.

The passion of your dreams
        reach out to the universe,
Gathering energy as they speed along,
        gaining momentum with every verse.

Looking deep within your eyes
reveals your greater Self within;
He has a secret he wants to share
and looks back at me with an impish grin.

His eyes sparkle with delight
as he watches the days go by,
And sees the daily strides you make
as you work to break inside.

He's having fun playing a game of hide-n-seek;
he sees you looking towards his hiding place
And stifles a child-like giggle
when you don't count him out at home base.

Yet, like the Genie in Aladdin's lamp,
he is anxiously waiting for you to find the key, in
order to set him free.
He wants you to use his power
to help fulfill your every need;

Just rub the lamp you're holding in your hands, close
your eyes and believe.

You stood and sent a silent message
hoping that I could hear.
One explaining your current passage,
so your intentions would be clear.

I heard your depth of feeling,
as you spoke your inner plea -
To leave the doors wide open
and allow the energies to flow free.

To feel the warmth flowing
back and forth between us;
To aid the strength that is growing
with no fear or worry of expectance.

I answered by stepping away from the threshold,
not knowing if you understood,
That I had not withdrawn or turned cold,
but was showing support the only way I could.

The doors are always opened wide
to a dear and treasured friend,
To offer retreat from the world outside
or simply lend a helping hand.

LOVE HURTS?

I often hear people say that love hurts –
but how can that possibly be true?
Love is an energy source that gives and receives
freely;
it has no sense of being blue.
It addresses the total connectedness between two
beings;
the physical, the spiritual, and emotional-
Weaving and intertwining the fibers of existence,
to share and bond with the joys of living.
Love extends it's fibers out into the universe,
attracting like energies; to guide and direct
what was always meant to be.
Love won't be bound by the confines of a script;
it has no concept of space or time.
It only knows the moment; only the present.
Fear within the surface is Love's mortal enemy,
and causes us the pain.
It instills doubts within the self
and demands focus on and worry for the future.
Fear diminishes the beauty and spontaneity
of the Love and forces it away by looking only at the
surface;
Only to gain a firmer grip by increasing it's own pain.

SPIRTUAL AND PHYSICAL LOVE

The night our spirits joined was the most incredible,
joy-filled experience of my life.
It was natural, unforced and totally unexpected. The
intensity was more than my inner essence could
handle, and the exquisiteness of the event extended to
my physical being. I felt the room spin and noticed I
was holding my breath. I felt my consciousness join
yours without losing sight of my physical
surroundings.

As I saw you walk through the door and take me in
your arms, my entire being started to shiver and
shake from the passion of the moment. The beauty
and incredible tenderness, mixed with a passion of
inexhaustible strength, caused tears of the purest love
imagined to pour from my eyes.
Your eyes probed the most intimate dimension of my
existence, and I forgot all else. I looked within your
spirit, sending forth and enveloping you in a shower of
energy. The radiance of the moment set my flesh on
fire, adding fuel to the union.

As our spirits exhausted themselves and satisfied the
craving within, my conscious self was also fulfilled,
and left feeling weak from the totality of the event.

The time is fast approaching
        for us to say goodbye,
And the bitter-sweet emotions I feel
        bring a tear of sorrow to my eye.

Your journey has taken you down a path
        that's sometimes hard to understand;
One requiring all new connections
        in place of my old, helping hand.

But to realize your higher Self
        is what I want most for you to find;
To feel free within and love yourself
        with your entire heart, soul and mind.

So I would much rather hurt on the surface
        and gladly let you go,
Than hurt you on a higher plane
        by trying to hold onto your soul.

But if the time should ever come
        and you need me once again,
I will always be there for you,
        to love and cherish you with welcoming hands.

SECTION II

LOVE EXPERIENCES

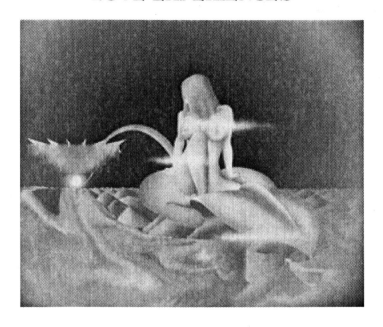

OF

NATURE

Shimmering lights upon the water
flowing in my direction,
Sending energy into my being
as I sit here in my solstice.

Choreographed dances of waves
putting on a show,
Exhibiting their vibrancy of life
and a radiance of their own.

I hear the song of the distant fall
caressing the stones below,
Running to join the massive lake
and share in it's grand performing show.

I'm invited to exchange energies
and find myself enveloped,
In the midst of it's softness
and unique soothing beauty.

A gentle breeze is touching my face,
lightly pushing back my hair.
It's coolness is a welcomed refrain
from the heat of the glorious sun.

A patch of powder-blue sky is visiting
in the guise of a butterfly;
Giving kisses upon my skin
checking to see if I'm all right.

And now, the sun is getting tired
and is preparing to go to bed.
The birds are following suit
by gathering one last snack.

One briefly stops beside me
and gives a melodic hello,
Before scampering back into the woods
  to feed it's young waiting in a hollow.

THE BODY'S PLEA

Do not deny me, the Body, because you think I am part of the Ego. I am just the opposite. I am that major aspect the Ego wants you to deny, because of the power and strength I contain. The Ego will have you believe that the Body is sinful and the root of all evil, when the Ego itself is to blame.

The Ego would have you believe it is sinful to give me pleasure; to please me; to be proud of me; to love me, only because the Ego knows that through me, you can access your very life force and enter worlds of beauty beyond belief.

You, your essence, selected me as your vehicle in this world. Through me, you experience the warmth of the sun upon your face; the magical wonder of touch itself. You wonder at the millions of textures you experience everyday, but did you remember that you are actually experiencing the glory of energy itself, expressing it's freedom and creativity as those textures?

Get to know me and the multitude of sensations you experience through me. Am I not a creative energy worthy of your attention and love? Examine your hair as though seeing it and touching it for the very first time. What color am I? Am I one solid color, or a multitude of colors blending into one?
Compare the texture of the hair on your head with the hair on your arms, your face, your stomach, your legs, your genitals. Are they all not different?

The Ego has no concept of creativity and is intent on blocking out your perceptions of the physical world around you. It is the Ego who tells you, you can't do something. Approximately only ten percent of my brain's capabilities are used. It is not I holding you back, it is the Ego fighting to maintain control, so you do not realize the power at your disposal. How many times have you tried something new and the experience "scared" you, so you either terminated the experience prematurely or decided never to try it again? The Ego is responsible for instilling the fear in you, to thwart any attempt to grow, become stronger, or simply experience life.

I, on the other hand, relish the feeling of exhilaration of new experiences. The surge of energy flowing all the way through me, opening the doors for yet more experiences.

The Ego has you convinced that you are separate from nature. The Ego says you are superior because you are "intelligent" and possess a soul. The Ego maintains that it's okay to destroy nature, as long as it is for the body's comfort and use, because of our "intelligence."
By getting to know me and love me, I can open the doors for you to experience and live the opposite. I can show you that all of nature is one, and everything around us not only has a consciousness, but it's own unique intelligence.

By putting the Ego to rest and opening yourself up to the full intensity of the energy I contain; by flowing freely with the sensations I can create, you will discover for yourself how shallow and contriving the Ego is.

54

Find a private, quiet park or meadow, or any other location where you feel at peace, and either sit or lie on the ground. Ignore anything the Ego tries to tell you and concentrate on listening to the surroundings. Block out everything else from your mind and simply utilize my sense of hearing. Pick out one sound and follow it wherever it goes. It will lead you to another sound. You may be listening to various species of birds, insects, leaves rustling in the wind; you are capable of listening to the sound of pure energy. Everything, including light and colors have their own unique symphony of sound. What may have started out as a "quiet" setting, will soon be brimming with music.

Next, concentrate on my touch sensations. Isolate one aspect of feeling, possibly the feel of a single blade of grass between your fingers, and allow yourself to experience the magnitude it has on me. Follow the energy of that sensation all the way through me; touching and affecting the very core of me. Now follow the sensation back to the original source and beyond. Not only have I allowed you feel the energy of the blade of grass coming into you, but I have also opened the door for you to feel our energy entering and flowing back through to the blade of grass.

Once you have learned to love me and open yourself up to me, you will experience the unity with nature. While you are lying in a field of grass, you may feel me, the Body, exchange energies with the earth; to become part of the earth. You will feel me sink into the ground below me and into nature itself. You may feel as though I disappeared and all that is left is your conscious energy. And here, lies the truth; the Body is one with nature and the energy of your essence; your consciousness is free to enter and explore whatever realm it wants.

Be aware of the games the Ego will try to play with you while you are learning to experience the total me. As you start to blend with nature, the exhilarating sensation of twirling around or becoming "bigger than life" may be new a experience for you, and the Ego may throw fear into you, scaring you into ending the experience prematurely. As I said before, the Ego doesn't want you to love me or get to know me, so it will try to send distracting thoughts to your mind, breaking your concentration. Simply acknowledge the distraction and then ignore it.

Even while making love, by flowing with, and accepting the total experience, and by following the energy to it's source, your two bodies may flow into one another and become one; disappearing together; leaving the joy and ecstasy of your radiant life force exploring and uniting with one another.

On the other hand, the Ego will try to force you to think only of performance and technique, robbing you of the free flowing pleasure waiting for you; convincing you that if you don't follow the book, you will fail as a lover. Again, the Ego doesn't want you to experience the passion of two energy sources joining together, expanding into the universe. The Ego can only gain control through feelings of failure, apathy, disappointment, resignation and works hard to perpetuate those less-than-happy emotions. It empowers itself with the energy you use when you argue with or berate yourself.

While you are relaxing at home, take a look at your surroundings and make note of what you see. You may think you are looking at a variety of stationary objects. Items such as pieces of furniture, the carpet, maybe a table. Possibly, you will notice a plant or two. Take note of the colors of all the objects you see.

I am going to tell you now that it is the Ego directing your perceptions of what you see. Think back to a time when you looked at a "solid" object and you thought you saw it move. The Ego convinced you that either your eyes were playing tricks on you because you were tired, or the lights and shadows were causing a hallucination. My dear friend, you were not seeing things. You were catching a glimpse of what is actually going on around you; what I am trying to show you. Nothing is solid. Everything is made up of atoms molecules moving freely in space, changing forms at will. The solidity you see is the hallucination.

I want nothing more than to have you trust me enough to show you the beauty of the world surrounding you. Everything is in a constant state of motion and creativity. You can observe that motion if you put the Ego to rest. There is a power you have access to, just through total, focused observation. Shift your consciousness and allow me to show you the choreography of motion and colors surrounding you on a daily basis. Lights dancing upon the floor in tune to their own music; the floor itself pretending it is an ocean wave keeping time, weaving back and forth, up and down, pretending it's the ocean's breath. Tell me, what did you notice, if anything, the last time you talked to your plants? Maybe you thought you saw them out of the corner of your eye waving to you, but dismissed the experience. Your plants are very sensitive, living creatures who respond positively to words of kindness and love, just as you do. When you talk to them, telling them how beautiful they are, they will start to shimmer and wave with excitement. Don't let the Ego convince you otherwise. Remember, I am your vehicle to experience *all* of reality.

Do you truly understand what happens when you meditate? Yes, you usually alter your state of consciousness and enter into an alpha state . . . But what happens before that? You concentrate on breathing deeply. When you breath deeply, you are filling every cell within me with oxygen, giving me the nourishment I need to help you experience your total reality. During the time you breath deeply and completely, the Ego is powerless. It cannot bully or rob energy from a rejuvenated body. That is why breathing deeply during times of extreme agitation or stress calms the nerves; you are giving me the nourishment required for smooth functioning. Think of it this way, shallow breathing provides the most minimal nourishment I require. It provides sustenance only. It's like only eating one light meal a day, without any supplemental vitamins. . . you can get by, but in no way are truly healthy and functioning at your utmost best.

When you give me the proper nutrition, you can't feel stress; only the joy of being, no matter what your circumstances are.

Take your time; don't rush it. I am your friend and your lover. Learn to please me without shame; celebrate me and take pride in me, for I am a direct reflection of you, for you chose me. Don't keep us separate; allow my life force to join with your consciousness and actively make an effort to allow your consciousness to join with my life force.

Before you know it, the Ego will wither away and die, because it will no longer be receiving the attention and energy it needs from you to keep control.

Do you still think I'm an extension of the Ego and deserve to be denied? Do you still think I cannot be creative? Just allow me the freedom to show you the mysteries of reality in such a creative fashion, you will be rejoicing in wonderment at being connected to this "mere" Body.

SEEING WITH NATURE'S EYES

Visiting with and walking in the woods always provided me with new lessons about life and nature, and revitalized the sense of "reality" within me. Every walk provided a new and unique experience.

This visit was no different. As promised, this adventure was unlike any other I had experienced, and yet, the beauty of it is difficult to explain or even comprehend. One could almost say it was awe inspiring.

On this day, the woods were calling to me to join them, indicating they had a birthday present for me. I was really surprised, since I had to miss my "birthday" walk due to extremely bad weather. They were shimmering with life and energy as they spoke to me, promising a beautiful experience. The point of entry into the woods was chosen for me; one I hadn't used before. Knowing something special was in store for me, I took several deep breaths before proceeding. I knew I had to step outside of myself in order to learn my lesson and receive the full benefit of the gift. As soon as I took my first step, the woods became vibrant with life! The sun was leading the way by directing it's beam first in spot and then another, leading me deeper and deeper into the woods.

I came across a sapling with a broken trunk. Someone had cared so strongly about that little tree that it had been bandaged in splints and a fresh dressing applied so it could heal. I stopped and sent healing energy into the tree, focusing on the break, to help it grain strength. It almost felt as though I literally stepped inside of the tree in order to share my energy with it. In turn, the little sapling sent appreciative energy back to me, as if to say, "Thank you."

When we finished exchanging energies, I realized the woods were buzzing with music. I heard the rush of a mountain stream coming from the left, even though I knew the woods did not contain a stream. At first, I thought I might be hearing traffic in the distance, but knew I wasn't. However, as soon as my mind focused on the word "traffic," I became acutely aware of it's sounds coming from a different direction. The awareness of the traffic disappeared, to make room for the sound of water drops hitting the ground, drumming out the rhythm of the heartbeat of the woods.

I took a few more steps along the path and was greeted by the Keeper of the Woods; a beautiful, yet powerful miniature dragon. As I approached closer, the dragon welcomed me to his domain, with promises of a truly unique adventure. I was now right next to the dragon, and I was filled with wonder to discover that in the surface world reality, it was a "dead" tree stump that had been blackened by lightening and had fallen over. However, the energy pouring from it confirmed that it was in no way "dead."

The dragon was very much alive, and fully aware and proud of it's post as Keeper. I knelt down beside it and asked if I may touch it. The dragon radiated with delight at the request and gladly gave permission. As I very lightly stroked the dragon's muzzle, the velvety smoothness and warm vibration emanating from it filled my eyes with tears of joy.

Suddenly, a blackbird flew into a nearby tree, telling me it was time for me to continue on my journey, and I followed his lead down the path. While I was walking along, drinking from the cup of nature's beauty, I realized I was witnessing the dance of atoms in the air. I could see I was surrounded within their energy and enveloped in warmth, even though the temperature itself was rather cool.

I felt as though I was walking within the woods as a part of the woods; not separate. I remember thinking, "This must be how a bird feels when it flies through the woods." I could no longer feel the solid ground beneath my feet; I felt I was walking on air. I could feel myself, my consciousness get larger; closer to the

62

size of the trees, then I felt as though I was no larger than a small rodent. This feeling of largeness then smallness continued as I gazed in wonderment at nature's miracles; The sun focusing it's rays on different trees, plants and rocks, to draw my attention to them. I felt as though I was in a protective room, looking at exquisite murals.

I turned down a fork in the path and was greeted by a single pine needle dancing in mid-air. The flowing, graceful movement of it's dance blocked out everything else. I was not aware of any trees close enough to be responsible for the needle's presence. As I approached closer, the pine needle told me it was my teacher for the day, and that my role was very simple; all I had to do was focus my attention on it's dance and flow with whatever I may witness around me.

The needle started to pirouette, sway back and forth, move in real close to me, fly towards the denser part of the woods away from me, and then return. I kept myself focused on the pine needle's dance, and at first, the rest of my surroundings totally disappeared. Then, I noticed the trees and the foliage had returned and were changing shape and colors, blending into one another; becoming separate again. I was aware that the distance between me and the heart of the woods was disappearing, coming within inches of my being. Within seconds, I was totally enveloped in a blanket of foliage. There was no empty space above me or around me. The woods were actually flowing through my mind and physical being, as though we were holograms. All the while, the pine needle continued dancing, joining the games of the woods, skipping in and out of their energy, while their energy continued to join with mine.

The pine needle then started to enter into the core of energy itself and wanted me to follow it. The speed of movement I experienced as I started to fly into energy's core literally made my head swim, frightening my physical being, and I was immediately brought back to "surface" reality. I knew my Ego was responsible for terminating the exhilarating adventure, instilling fear in me. The pine needle reassured me that it was okay, and we would just continue.

I have no concept of how long these exercises continued. I learned that I could close the gap of space itself; that space is as much of an illusion as time. I continued walking through the woods long after the lessons were over, shifting my focus on the true nature of the woods. The trees, plants and bushes would blend together, forming a continuous wall of color and design. It reminded me of the stereogram I have at home before I would shift focus to see the eagle inside. From that scene, the woods would then start changing to form their own image inside of the "print." They created various dancing swirls of lines, and geometric shapes became apparent. Again, I felt I was in the midst of a living hologram.

The melodious songs of the birds flying overhead told me it was now time to end my visit. I was walking along the path back home when I saw a magnificent tree that had been uprooted, due to age or a storm, and was lying on the ground. The fine, delicate artwork of the roots formed a natural latticework that gave the image of full-ground trees in miniature. They called out to me, and I asked if I may please take a part of them home. They told me since I asked the question, I already knew the answer, and two strands of artwork magically dropped into my hands, filling me with inspired energy. In that moment, I could see an incredible 3-D painting form in my mind. Throughout my journey leaving the woods, I was still focused in that reality, and was instructed to bring home a couple of other items to include in the painting.

I encountered the Keeper again and thanked him for the beautiful birthday present. He started smiling and shook his head up and down. I told him I would like to come back and take a picture of him when I had some film, and he indicated the gesture would please him very much.

I walked by the tree with the splint and told him he was going to make it and he again thanked me for the healing energy I gave him.

Coming out of the woods and walking back to my apartment was an experience of it's own. In one sense, I felt very heavy and had to get used to my "land" legs again. Changing my visual focus back to the surface reality of the Ego was very difficult. My eyes became very sore and irritated from the strain, and it took a couple of days for my eyes to clear up.

This was why the weather had changed for the worse on my birthday; I would not have been able to report to work directly after this experience. The muscles in my eyes were stiff and sore from the adventure, much like the way other muscles become stiff and sore when they're not used to exercise.

I decided to go to sleep as soon as I got home, in order to give my eyes a much needed rest, but tried an experiment of own before drifting off to sleep. I shifted my waking consciousness and focused on closing the physical gap between myself and my loved one in a different state. The space closed up and it felt as though he was actually in the next room. The last thing I remember was my teacher telling me that that was part of my lesson; two people united can be together not only on a psychic, spiritual level simply feeling each other's presence emotionally, but can close the gap of space as we know it, and *physically* feel the closeness as well.

REWARDS

On my way to my favorite meditation spot, I heard a voice say, "Quick! Pull over here, now!"
I complied and stopped the car, looking for the source. I peered over a ridge several yards from the road, and saw a couple of trees standing alone on the other side of a creek. They called to me to come on down, that they wanted to give me a gift.

My steps down the ridge and across the creek were guided by Mother Earth herself - keeping my steps firm and steady so that I may reach my destination safe and sound.

As I approached the base of the trees, I instinctively looked upon the ground and saw my treasure smiling up at me, and I knew this was the voice I had heard. The power and energy were unmistakable, as I reached down to pick it up. The shape of the stone was that of a mallard's head, and there, on the stone itself, Nature had painted the head of an eaglet begging for food.

Earlier in the day, I was wishing to myself that, for just once, I would like to find a stone or a piece of wood that resembled a bird. Since I have so many birds at home, and many people referred to me a the "Bird Goddess" it was natural for me to look for natural shapes of birds whenever I went for a walk in the woods or along the lake. I was thinking how magical it was to have my wish come true so quickly!

Gazing upon and feeling the stone's natural beauty, it twinkled with energy and told me I was in for a surprise. Wondering what it meant, I crossed back over the creek and walked back to my car. I was presented with another gift as I was driving out of the park. A red-tailed hawk appeared out of nowhere and crossed over me, making eye-contact. Then, without warning, it did a flip in the air and poured a bucket of energy over my head, filling me to the brim. It then stayed with me, flying along the side of the car, as if I was taking it for a walk, as an omen of many good things to come throughout my life.

EVERYTHING IS BEAUTIFUL

Today, I was drawn to the park all the while at work. The mountains and the trees were calling to me, like a million voices joining together in harmony. When I could no longer resist their persistent call, I left work and headed straight for the choir. The essence of pure tranquillity enveloped my being, as I was immersed in the kaleidoscope of leaves turning in the afternoon fog.

During my journey, I witnessed a mist of clouds descend and embrace the awaiting woods and mountains, like a gentle lover. The clouds caressed the park ever so attentively, so as to allow the sun's warming rays to shine through to pre-chosen spots. The surrealistic array of orange, yellow, green and red sent my senses reeling. I held my breath as I was pulled into the totality of it's beauty. The energy was too great for words. It seemed to transfer to the car, as it accelerated without my aid to reach our destination without delay.

The sweetness of the air brought out nature's wonders to feast on the bounty. I was embraced by the sound of magpies singing to the rain, a black bear taking her cubs for a walk in the mist, and a family of white tailed deer dining out in the wilderness. I was graced by the totality of the universe and all it's splendid wonder.

Majestic mountains all around
reaching to the sky.
Glorious sun playing peek-a-boo
as pillows of clouds twirl by.

Ponderosa pines swaying to the beat
of the orchestra of the wind,
Challenging themselves to a game of limbo
to see how low they can bend.

Wild turkeys landing in the meadow
looking for a place to rest,
Dance to the tune of Turkey in the Straw
while a cock exhibits his best.

Healing steam from the hot springs
envelops the midnight air,
Creating a mystical illusion
of spirits romping here.

Constellations turning on their lights
write your name to celebrate your birth.
They're creating a cake from the glitter of stardust
and sprinkling it upon the earth.

The magic of the stardust
is now at your command,
For it sent it's energy and power
onto the page you're now holding in your hands.

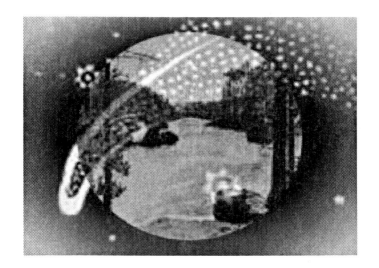

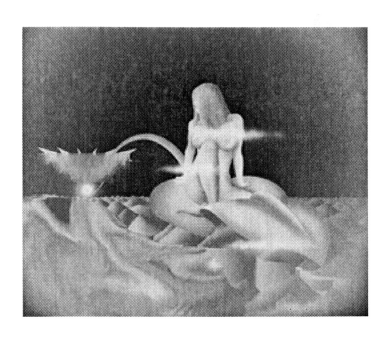

About the author

To G. Shanier, Gloria Clark to those who know her, the world has always been divided into two sections; the Surface World and the Second World, which is driven by the heartbeat of Mother Earth and the deep inner energies of the universe. By quieting the day-to-day surface conversations and situations reliving themselves inside her head, she is able to "let go" and allow the honest, love energies to come through and see beyond the surface facades. Her pen name, G. Shanier, is representative of putting the Ego aside in order to *"seek within . . . flow without."*

By listening with her "inner" ear and focusing with her "inner" eyes, she is able to communicate with and appreciate the incredible creative force we call nature. She has lived her entire live in the Rocky Mountain region, and currently resides in Columbia Falls, Montana.